CROTCHET MADE EASY

A GUIDE TO CROTCHETING

AMANDA WILLIAMS

Copyright
Copying or reproducing this book without the author's permission is prohibited (© 2025).

Table of Contents

INTRODUCTION TO CROCHETING 11
    THE WORLD OF CROCHETING 11
    A BRIEF HISTORY OF CROCHETING 11
    THE TOOLS OF THE TRADE 13
    UNDERSTANDING YARN LABELS 13
    HOLDING YOUR HOOK AND YARN................... 14
    THE JOY OF CROCHETING............................... 18

CHAPTER 2 19
    BASIC STITCHES AND TECHNIQUES................... 19
        THE FOUNDATION OF CROCHETING: BASIC STITCHES... 19
        UNDERSTANDING STITCHES AND THEIR ROLE 19
        THE BASIC STITCHES 21
        PRACTICING BASIC STITCHES 25
        HOW TO READ A CROCHET PATTERN............ 26
        TROUBLESHOOTING COMMON ISSUES.......... 28
        PRACTICE MAKES PERFECT 30

CHAPTER 3 32
    STARTING YOUR FIRST CROCHET PROJECT 32
        CHOOSING YOUR FIRST PROJECT 32

2. SELECTING MATERIALS FOR YOUR PROJECT 34

3. UNDERSTANDING PATTERNS AND INSTRUCTIONS 36

4. PREPARING TO CROCHET 37

5. STEP-BY-STEP GUIDE TO MAKING A DISHCLOTH 38

6. TIPS FOR SUCCESS 41

7. TROUBLESHOOTING COMMON ISSUES 42

8. COMPLETING YOUR FIRST PROJECT 43

9. LOOKING AHEAD 43

CHAPTER 4 45

EXPLORING PATTERNS, TEXTURES AND STITCH VARIATIONS 45

1. THE IMPORTANCE OF PATTERNS AND TEXTURES IN CROCHET 45

2. READING AND UNDERSTANDING CROCHET PATTERN CHART 47

HOW TO READ A CROCHET CHART 47

3. INTRODUCING TEXTURED STITCHES 48

Post stitches front and back 50

4. COMBINING STITCHES TO CREATE PATTERNS 51

5. EXPLORING COLORWORK TECHNIQUES ...53

6. Planning and Executing a Textured Project .54

7. Tips for Success with Patterns and Textures ..55

8. Troubleshooting Challenges in Textured Work 56

9. Expanding Your Creativity 57

10. Looking Ahead 57

CHAPTER 5 59

PATTERNS, TECHNIQUES , TEXTURES...............59

1 READING CROCHET PATTERNS....................59

2 WORKING IN ROWS VS. ROUNDS 62

3 CREATING BASIC SHAPES............................64

4 ADDING TEXTURE WITH STITCHES 66

5 COMBINING PATTERNS AND TEXTURES.....68

6 ADVANCED TECHNIQUES 68

CHAPTER 6 70

CRAFTING CROCHET PROJECTS FOR EVERY SKILL LEVEL 70

1 THE BASICS OF PLANNING CROCHET PROJECTS 70

2 BEGINNER PROJECTS: BUILDING CONFIDENCE..73

3 INTERMEDIATE PROJECTS: EXPANDING YOUR SKILLS 75

4. ADVANCED PROJECTS: PUSHING YOUR LIMITS..78

- 5 CUSTOMIZING YOUR PROJECTS 80
- 6 TROUBLESHOOTING AND FINISHING TECHNIQUES 81

CHAPTER 7 84
CARING FOR CROCHET CREATIONS AND SHARING YOUR CRAFT 84
- 1 CARING FOR CROCHET ITEMS 84
  - STORING CROCHET ITEMS 87
  - REPAIRING CROCHET ITEMS 88
- 2 GIFTING CROCHET CREATIONS 89
- 3 SELLING YOUR CROCHET WORK 91
  - SETTING UP YOUR CROCHET BUSINESS 91
  - SELLING ONLINE 93
  - SELLING LOCALLY 94
- 4 JOINING THE CROCHET COMMUNITY 94

CHAPTER 8 97
TROUBLESHOOTING COMMON CROCHET PROBLEMS 97
- 1. WHY MISTAKES HAPPEN IN CROCHET 98
- 2. COMMON CROCHET PROBLEMS AND HOW TO FIX THEM 99
- 3 DEALING WITH FRUSTRATION IN CROCHET 106

6. LEARNING TO EMBRACE IMPERFECTION 107
7. MOVING FORWARD AND BUILDING CONFIDENCE 107
CONCLUSION 108

INTRODUCTION

Crocheting is a versatile and creative craft that involves using a hooked needle, called a crochet hook, to interlock loops of yarn, thread, or other materials into a wide variety of patterns and designs. It is an art form that dates back centuries and has evolved into a popular pastime and practical skill. Crocheting is cherished for its ability to produce handmade items ranging from functional pieces like blankets, clothing, and bags to decorative items such as doilies, toys, and intricate lacework.The process begins with a foundation chain of loops, which serves as the base for creating rows or rounds of stitches. These stitches come in various forms, including single crochet, double crochet, treble crochet, and more, each contributing unique textures and designs to the finished piece. By combining stitches in different sequences, crafters can produce intricate patterns, textures, and shapes.Crocheting is also highly accessible. It requires minimal tools—typically just a crochet hook, yarn, and scissors—making it a portable and affordable hobby. Yarn comes in various weights, textures, and colors, allowing endless creative possibilities for projects. The craft is suitable for all skill levels, from beginners learning basic stitches to experienced crocheters tackling complex patterns and advanced techniques such as Tunisian crochet or tapestry crochet.One of the most appealing aspects of crocheting is its meditative and therapeutic qualities. The repetitive motion of stitching can reduce stress, improve focus, and promote relaxation. Many people find joy and fulfillment in creating something tangible with their hands, and crocheting offers a sense of accomplishment as projects come to life. Crocheting also fosters a strong sense of community. Enthusiasts often gather in groups, both online and in person, to share patterns, techniques, and inspiration. Many crocheters create. handmade gifts for loved ones or contribute to charitable causes by crafting items such as blankets, hats, and scarves for those in need.

CHAPTER 1

INTRODUCTION TO CROCHETING

THE WORLD OF CROCHETING

Crocheting is more than just a craft—it's an art form, a therapeutic hobby, and a practical skill that allows you to create beautiful, functional, and meaningful items from yarn or thread. Whether you're new to crafting or an experienced DIY enthusiast, crocheting opens up a world of creative possibilities that can be tailored to your skill level and interests. This chapter will introduce you to the fundamentals of crocheting, covering its history, tools, and materials, as well as essential techniques like holding your hook and yarn.

A BRIEF HISTORY OF CROCHETING

Crocheting has a fascinating history, believed to date back centuries. While the exact origins remain unclear, many historians trace the craft to early forms of needlework practiced in regions such as Arabia, South America, and China. However, crocheting in its modern form began to gain popularity in Europe during the 19th century. During this time, crocheting became a widespread pastime, particularly among women in Victorian England. It was often used to replicate the intricate lace patterns that were highly valued at the time. Unlike machine-made lace, crocheted lace offered a personal, handmade touch, making it a symbol of creativity and care.

In the 20th century, crocheting evolved beyond lacework to include a wide range of practical and decorative items. The craft saw a resurgence during the 1960s and 1970s, when bold colors and freeform crochet became synonymous with the counterculture movement. Today, crocheting continues to thrive as both a traditional craft and a modern art form, embraced by people of all ages and backgrounds.

THE TOOLS OF THE TRADE

- Yarn Needle: Also called a tapestry needle, this tool is used for weaving in loose ends or sewing pieces together.
- Row Counters: A useful gadget for tracking your progress in larger or more detailed projects.

UNDERSTANDING YARN LABELS

When you purchase yarn, the label contains important information that will guide you in selecting the right materials for your project. Key details include:

- Fiber Content: Indicates whether the yarn is made of wool, cotton, acrylic, or other fibers.
- Weight: Identifies the thickness of the yarn (e.g., DK, worsted, bulky).
- Hook Size Recommendation: Suggests an appropriate crochet hook size for the yarn.

- Gauge: Specifies the number of stitches and rows per inch to achieve a specific tension.
- Care Instructions: Provides guidance on washing and maintaining your finished piece.

HOLDING YOUR HOOK AND YARN

Learning how to hold your crochet hook and yarn is one of the first steps in mastering the craft. While there's no single "right" way to do it, finding a method that feels comfortable and natural to you is key.

Holding the Hook

There are two common ways to hold a crochet hook:
- Pencil Grip: Hold the hook as you would a pencil, with your thumb and index finger controlling its movement.
- Knife Grip: Hold the hook as you would a knife, with your palm facing downward and your thumb and fingers gripping the handle.

Experiment with both grips to see which one suits you best. Some people find one grip more ergonomic than the other, especially for extended crocheting sessions.

Holding the Yarn

Your non-dominant hand controls the yarn tension and guides it into the hook.
1. Wrap the yarn around your fingers to maintain consistent tension.
2. For beginners, a common method is to loop the yarn over your pinky, under your ring and middle fingers, and over your index finger. This creates enough tension to keep the yarn taut while allowing it to move freely.

Maintaining even tension is critical for creating consistent stitches and a polished finished product. Practice holding the yarn until it feels natural and intuitive.

Getting Started: Forming a Slipknot

The first step in any crochet project is creating a slipknot to attach the yarn to your hook. Here's how to do it:

1. Make a loop with the yarn, crossing the working yarn (the end attached to the ball) over the tail.

2. Insert your hook into the loop and grab the working yarn with the hook.

3. Pull the working yarn through the loop, tightening it to form a knot. Your slipknot should be snug around the hook but loose enough to slide easily.

The Foundation Chain

The foundation chain is the starting point for most crochet projects. It consists of a series of chain stitches (abbreviated as "ch" in patterns). To create a chain stitch:

1. Yarn over (wrap the yarn around the hook).

2. Pull the yarn through the loop on your hook.

Repeat these steps to create the desired number of chain stitches for your project. The foundation chain should be even and not too tight, as this can affect the overall appearance and flexibility of your work.

Tips for Beginners

Starting a new craft can feel overwhelming, but with practice and patience, you'll build confidence and skill. Here are some tips to set yourself up for success:

1. . Start Small: Choose simple projects like dishcloths, scarves, or coasters to practice basic stitches.
2. Medium-Weight Yarn and a Larger Hook: These materials are easier to work with and help you see your stitches more clearly.
3. Practice Consistent Tension: Focus on keeping your stitches even, neither too tight nor too loose.
4. Take Breaks: Crocheting for long periods can strain your hands and

wrists, so take regular breaks to stretch and rest.

Be Patient: Mistakes are a natural part of learning. Don't be discouraged if your first projects aren't perfect—each one is a step toward improvement.

THE JOY OF CROCHETING

As you embark on your crocheting journey, remember that this craft is as much about the process as it is about the finished product. Crocheting offers an opportunity to slow down, focus on the present moment, and express your creativity. Whether you're making gifts for loved ones, decorating your home, or simply enjoying the act of stitching, crocheting is a rewarding and fulfilling activity that can bring joy and satisfaction for years to come.By now, you should have a good understanding of the craft's history, tools, and basic techniques. In the next chapter, you'll learn about the foun

CHAPTER 2

BASIC STITCHES AND TECHNIQUES

THE FOUNDATION OF CROCHETING: BASIC STITCHES

Crocheting is built on a series of foundational stitches that serve as the building blocks for virtually every project. Mastering these stitches is essential for anyone starting their crochet journey. In this chapter, we'll guide you step-by-step through the most fundamental stitches—chain stitch, single crochet, double crochet, and slip stitch—and introduce you to the techniques needed to read patterns and begin your projects.

UNDERSTANDING STITCHES AND THEIR ROLE

Each crochet stitch creates a unique texture, appearance, and functionality. The beauty of crocheting lies in its simplicity: even the most intricate designs are made by combining a few basic stitches in creative ways. Once you've learned the essentials, you'll have the foundation to explore more advanced patterns and techniques.

Before diving into the stitches, it's important to understand some key terms and concepts:

1.Working Yarn: The strand of yarn attached to your yarn ball or skein. This is the yarn you manipulate to form stitches.

2.Loops on the Hook: At any given time, your crochet hook will have at least one loop on it. This loop is the foundation for creating new stitches.

3.Yarn Over (YO): A fundamental motion in crocheting where you wrap the working yarn around your hook, either from back to front or in the direction indicated in the pattern.

THE BASIC STITCHES

1. Chain Stitch (ch): The chain stitch is the simplest and most fundamental stitch in crochet. It forms the foundation chain, which acts as the starting point for most crochet projects.

Steps to Create a Chain Stitch:

- Begin with a slipknot on your hook.
- Hold the hook in your dominant hand and the working yarn in your non-dominant hand.
- Yarn over (wrap the yarn around the hook).
- Pull the yarn through the loop on your hook.

Repeat this process to create additional chains. Each chain should be even in size, and they should not be too tight, as this can make the foundation chain difficult to work into.

Tips for Success:

- Practice keeping consistent tension in your yarn to ensure all chains are uniform.
- If your chain is too tight, use a larger hook until you feel comfortable.

2. Single Crochet (sc): The single crochet is one of the most commonly used stitches. It creates a dense, durable fabric that's perfect for items like dishcloths, coasters, or amigurumi (crocheted stuffed toys).

Steps to Create a Single Crochet:

- Insert your hook into the next stitch or chain.
- Yarn over and pull up a loop (you should now have two loops on your hook).
- Yarn over again and pull through both loops on your hook.

Repeat these steps to continue making single crochet stitches across your row.

Common Uses:

- Single crochet stitches are often used for tight, sturdy designs.
- They're ideal for beginners because they're easy to learn and control.

3. Double Crochet (dc): The double crochet stitch is taller than the single crochet, creating a looser, more open fabric. It's versatile and commonly used in patterns for blankets, shawls, and garments.

Steps to Create a Double Crochet:

- Yarn over before inserting your hook into the next stitch or chain.
- Insert your hook into the stitch and yarn over, pulling up a loop (you should now have three loops on your hook).
- Yarn over again and pull through the first two loops (you should now have two loops on your hook).
- Yarn over one last time and pull through the remaining two loops.

Repeat this process to create additional double crochet stitches.

Key Features:

- Double crochet stitches are taller and faster to work than single crochets.
- They create a more open and airy texture, making them great for lightweight or decorative items.

4. Slip Stitch (sl st): The slip stitch is a short, compact stitch used for joining pieces, finishing edges, or moving across a row without adding height.

Steps to Create a Slip Stitch:

- Insert your hook into the desired stitch or chain.
- Yarn over and pull the yarn through both the stitch and the loop on your hook.

When to Use Slip Stitches:

- To join two pieces of crochet together.
- To create seamless rounds in circular projects like hats or granny squares.
- To add subtle detailing or edging.

PRACTICING BASIC STITCHES

To develop muscle memory and build confidence, practice creating swatches of each stitch. Start with a foundation chain of 15–20 stitches, then work several rows of single crochet, double crochet, or slip stitches. Pay attention to the tension, evenness, and appearance of your stitches as you go.

Combining Stitches

Once you're comfortable with individual stitches, you can start combining them to create patterns and textures. For example:

- Alternating Rows: Work one row of single crochet followed by one row of double crochet. This creates a visually interesting pattern with varying heights.

- Granny Squares: These are made by combining chains, double crochet stitches, and slip stitches to form decorative squares.

Experiment with different combinations to explore the versatility of these basic stitches.

HOW TO READ A CROCHET PATTERN

Crochet patterns are a set of instructions that guide you through the process of creating a specific design. They use standardized abbreviations, symbols, and diagrams to communicate the steps efficiently.

Common Abbreviations:

- ch = chain

- sc = single crochet

- dc = double crochet
- sl st = slip stitch
- st = stitch
- YO = yarn over

Sample Pattern:

Here's a simple example to demonstrate how patterns are written:

Pattern:

- Ch 21 (foundation chain).

- Row 1: Sc in the 2nd chain from the hook and in each chain across (20 sc). Turn.

- Row 2: Ch 2 (counts as dc), dc in each sc across. Turn.

- Row 3: Ch 1, sc in each dc across.

This pattern alternates rows of single and double crochet to create a textured swatch.

Reading Symbols: Some crochet patterns use stitch diagrams, which visually represent the stitches as symbols. This is especially useful for intricate or lace-like designs.

TROUBLESHOOTING COMMON ISSUES

As a beginner, it's normal to encounter challenges while learning basic stitches. Here are some common issues and tips for resolving them:

1. Uneven Tension:

   - Problem: Stitches vary in size, creating an uneven fabric.
   - Solution: Practice holding your yarn consistently and avoid pulling too tightly.

2. Missed Stitches:

   - Problem: Your row has fewer stitches than intended.

- Solution: Count your stitches at the end of each row and ensure you're working into the last stitch.

3. Too Tight Foundation Chain:

- Problem: The starting chain is tighter than the rest of your work.
- Solution: Use a larger hook for the foundation chain or consciously keep your tension loose.

4. Twisted Chains:

- Problem: Your foundation chain twists as you work into it.
- Solution: Lay the chain flat and ensure all stitches face the same direction before starting your first row.

Building Confidence with Simple Projects

Once you've mastered basic stitches, apply your skills to beginner-friendly projects. These can include:

- Dishcloths: Use single crochet stitches to make a small, square dishcloth.
- Scarves: Create a simple scarf by working rows of double crochet.
- Coasters: Practice working in the round with slip stitches and single crochets.

These projects will give you a sense of accomplishment while helping you refine your technique.

PRACTICE MAKES PERFECT

Crocheting, like any skill, improves with consistent practice. Dedicate time each day to work on your stitches, even if it's just for 15–30 minutes. Over time, your hands will become more comfortable with the motions, and your stitches will become more consistent.

The Joy of Progress

As you learn the basic stitches and techniques, take pride in your progress.

Each new skill you master brings you closer to creating intricate patterns and beautiful finished pieces. Crocheting is a journey of discovery, and this chapter marks the first step toward unlocking your creative potential.

CHAPTER 3

STARTING YOUR FIRST CROCHET PROJECT

Now that you've learned the basic stitches and techniques in Chapter 2, it's time to embark on your first crochet project. This chapter will guide you through selecting a beginner-friendly project, gathering materials, reading a pattern, and completing a simple design. By the end of this chapter, you'll not only have a finished crochet piece but also the confidence to tackle more complex projects in the future

CHOOSING YOUR FIRST PROJECT

Selecting your first project is an exciting step, but it's essential to start with something manageable. As a beginner, your first crochet project should focus on practicing your basic stitches and building confidence.

Ideal First Projects for Beginners

- Dishcloths: Small and simple, dishcloths allow you to practice stitches without committing to a large or complicated project.
- Scarves: A straight, rectangular scarf helps you master rows and consistency.
- Coasters: Coasters are small, quick projects that introduce you to working in the round.
- Headbands: A simple headband is a great way to practice tension and stitch repetition.

Key Considerations for Beginners

- Time Commitment: Choose a project that can be completed in a few hours or days to avoid frustration.
- Skill Level: Look for patterns labeled as "beginner" or "easy."
- Functionality: Select something practical that you'll enjoy using or

gifting, such as a scarf or a set of coasters.

2. SELECTING MATERIALS FOR YOUR PROJECT

The right materials can make your first crochet experience smoother and more enjoyable. Let's break down what you'll need.

Yarn

- Type: Acrylic yarn is a beginner's best friend—it's affordable, easy to work with, and widely available. Avoid slippery or textured yarns like silk or boucle for your first project.
- Weight: Choose a medium-weight yarn (labeled as "#4" or "worsted weight"). This yarn is versatile and easy to see while crocheting.
- Color: Select a light or medium-colored yarn, as dark or variegated

yarns can make it difficult to see your stitches.

Hook

- Size: For worsted weight yarn, a hook size of 5.5mm (I/9) or 6.0mm (J/10) is ideal for beginners. Larger hooks make it easier to see and manipulate stitches.
- Material: Aluminum hooks are smooth and affordable, making them a great choice for beginners.

Additional Tools

- Scissors: A sharp pair of scissors is essential for cutting yarn.
- Stitch Markers: These help you keep track of your place in a pattern.
- Measuring Tape: Useful for ensuring your project is the right size.
- Yarn Needle: A blunt-tipped needle for weaving in ends.

3. UNDERSTANDING PATTERNS AND INSTRUCTIONS

Reading a crochet pattern can feel overwhelming at first, but it's a skill that becomes second nature with practice.

Breaking Down a Pattern

Crochet patterns are written in a shorthand format using abbreviations and symbols. Here's what you'll typically find:

- Materials Section: Lists the required yarn, hook size, and any additional tools.
- Gauge: Indicates the number of stitches and rows needed to achieve a specific measurement (e.g., 4 inches by 4 inches). Matching gauge is essential for projects like clothing.
- Pattern Instructions: Step-by-step guidance for completing the project.

Common Abbreviations

- ch: Chain, sc: Single Crochet, dc: Double Crochet, sl st: Slip Stitch, st: Stitch

Sample Pattern

Let's look at a basic dishcloth pattern:

Pattern:

- Ch 26.
- Row 1: Sc in the 2nd ch from the hook and in each ch across (25 sc). Turn.
- Row 2: Ch 1, sc in each st across. Turn.
- Repeat Row 2 until the piece measures 8inches.
- Fasten off and weave in ends.

4. PREPARING TO CROCHET

Before you begin, it's essential to set yourself up for success.

Creating a Comfortable Workspace

- Find a well-lit area where you can see your stitches clearly.
- Sit in a comfortable chair with good back support.
- Keep your materials organized and within reach.

Practicing the Basics: Spend a few minutes practicing your chain stitch and single crochet to warm up and get comfortable with the motions.

5. STEP-BY-STEP GUIDE TO MAKING A DISHCLOTH

For this chapter, we'll walk you through a simple dishcloth project.

Materials Needed

- Worsted weight yarn (100% cotton is ideal for dishcloths).
- 5.5mm (I/9) crochet hook.
- Scissors, yarn needle, and measuring tape.

Instructions

Step 1: Create a Slipknot

- Make a loop with the yarn, crossing the working yarn over the tail.
- Insert your hook into the loop and pull the working yarn through to create a slipknot.
- Tighten the knot around the hook, ensuring it's snug but not too tight.

Step 2: Make a Foundation Chain

- Yarn over and pull through the loop on your hook to create a chain.
- Repeat until you have 26 chains.

Step 3: Work the First Row

- Insert your hook into the second chain from the hook (not the one directly next to it).
- Yarn over and pull up a loop (two loops on the hook).

- Yarn over again and pull through both loops to complete a single crochet.

Step 4: Continue Rows

- At the end of the row, chain 1 and turn your work.
- .Single crochet in each stitch across, working into the top loops of the stitches from the previous row.

Step 5: Finish the Dishcloth

- Continue working rows of single crochet until the piece measures 8 inches.
- Fasten off by cutting the yarn, leaving a 6-inch tail. Pull the tail through the loop on your hook and tighten to secure.

Step 6: Weave in Ends

- Thread the yarn needle with the tail and weave it through the stitches along the edge of the dishcloth.

- Trim any excess yarn.

6.TIPS FOR SUCCESS

Crocheting your first project can be a learning experience, so don't worry if it's not perfect. Here are some tips to help you succeed:

- Count Your Stitches: Regularly count the stitches in each row to ensure you haven't added or missed any.
- Use Stitch Markers: Place markers at the beginning and end of rows to keep your edges straight.
- Practice Tension: Focus on keeping your stitches even in size. If they're too tight or too loose, adjust your grip on the yarn.
- Take Breaks: Avoid hand and wrist strain by taking regular breaks to stretch.

7. TROUBLESHOOTING COMMON ISSUES

Uneven Edges

- Problem: Your dishcloth has wavy or uneven edges.
- Solution: Ensure you're working into the correct number of stitches in each row and use a stitch marker to mark the last stitch.

Gaps Between Stitches

- Problem: There are noticeable gaps in your fabric.
- Solution: Check that you're inserting your hook into the correct part of each stitch and maintaining consistent tension.

Crooked Rows

- Problem: Your rows are slanting or uneven.

- Solution : Make sure you're chaining the correct number of stitches at the beginning of each row and turning your work properly.

8. COMPLETING YOUR FIRST PROJECT

Finishing your first crochet project is a moment of pride! Take time to admire your work, even if it's not perfect. Remember, every stitch is a step toward improvement.

Celebrate Your Success

- Share your project with friends or family.
- Use your dishcloth and enjoy the satisfaction of a handmade item.
- Reflect on what you learned and think about your next project.

9. LOOKING AHEAD

Now that you've completed your first project, you're ready to explore more advanced techniques and patterns. By following these steps, you've not only completed a project but also built the foundation for a lifelong skill. Happy crocheting!

CHAPTER 4

EXPLORING PATTERNS, TEXTURES AND STITCH VARIATIONS

As you advance in your crochet journey, it's time to step beyond the basics and explore the vast creative potential of patterns, textures, and stitch variations. Chapter 4 focuses on deepening your skills, learning how to add visual interest to your work, and tackling projects that challenge and inspire you. This chapter will also guide you in understanding pattern charts, working with textured stitches, and combining stitch variations for unique designs.

1. THE IMPORTANCE OF PATTERNS AND TEXTURES IN CROCHET

Crochet is more than just functional; it's an art form. Patterns and textures elevate even the simplest designs, transforming ordinary projects into extraordinary works of craftsmanship. Here's why mastering textures and stitch variations is so rewarding:

- **Asthetic Appeal :** Patterns and textures add visual interest and dimension, making your projects stand out.
- **Versatility**: Combining stitch variations enables you to create a wide range of designs, from lacy shawls to chunky blankets.
- **Skill development**: Learning new patterns and textures expands your crochet repertoire, helping you tackle advanced projects.

This chapter introduces you to new techniques while teaching you how to read pattern charts and incorporate stitch variations seamlessly.

2. READING AND UNDERSTANDING CROCHET PATTERN CHART

Patterns are often written as text, but many include charts to visually represent the design. Crochet charts use symbols to illustrate stitches, making it easier to visualize the final result. Learning to read charts is a valuable skill that will open up new creative possibilities.

HOW TO READ A CROCHET CHART

Understanding the Layout

- Crochet charts are typically read from bottom to top, with the first row at the bottom of the chart.
- For rows: Read even-numbered rows from left to right and odd-numbered rows from right to left.
- For rounds: Read in a spiral direction, starting at the center.

Common Symbols

Each stitch has a corresponding symbol. Here are a few examples:

- Chain (ch): A small oval or circle.
- Single Crochet (sc): An "X" or a "+."
- Double Crochet (dc): A tall "T" with a horizontal line in the middle.
- Slip Stitch (sl st): A small dot.

Practice Example

Start with a simple chart for a granny square or a shell stitch. Follow the symbols step-by-step to create the design.

3. INTRODUCING TEXTURED STITCHES

Textured stitches are an exciting way to add depth and dimension to your crochet work. They create raised or recessed designs that make your projects visually interesting and tactile.

Popular Textured Stitches

Bobble Stitch

- Description: Creates small, rounded "bobbles" that add a playful texture

How-To

- Yarn over, insert hook into the stitch, yarn over again, and pull up a loop (three loops on the hook).
- Yarn over, pull through two loops.
- Repeat steps 1–2 four more times in the same stitch (you'll have six loops on the hook).
- Yarn over and pull through all six loops.

Popcorn Stitch

- Description : Similar to the bobble stitch but creates a denser, more pronounced texture.

How -To:

- Work 5 double crochet stitches into the same stitch.

- Remove your hook from the loop and insert it into the first double crochet of the group.
- Pull the loop through to close the "popcorn."

Cluster Stitch

Description: Groups multiple stitches together to form a raised, decorative effect

   •How-To:

- Yarn over, insert hook into stitch, and pull up a loop.
- Repeat the process in the same stitch multiple times (usually three or four).
- Yarn over and pull through all loops on the hook.

Post stitches front and back

- Description : Creates raised ridges by working around the post (the vertical part) of a stitch rather than into the top loops.

How-To:

- Front Post Double Crochet (FPdc): Yarn over, insert hook from front to back around the post, yarn over, and complete a double crochet.
- Back Post Double Crochet (BPdc): Yarn over, insert hook from back to front around the post, yarn over, and complete a double crochet.

4. COMBINING STITCHES TO CREATE PATTERNS

By combining basic and textured stitches, you can create intricate patterns and designs. Here are a few popular patterns to try:

1. Shell Stitch

- Description : Creates a scalloped, fan-like pattern.

How-To:

- Work 5 double crochet stitches into the same stitch.
- .Skip the next two stitches and secure the shell with a single crochet.
- .Repeat across the row.

2. Basketweave Stitch

- Description:: Mimics the look of woven fabric using front and back post stitches.

How-To:

- Alternate two front post double crochets (FPdc) and two back post double crochets (BPdc) across the row.
- On the next row, reverse the order to create the woven texture.

3. Ripple or Chevron Pattern

Description:: Features a zigzag or wave-like design.

How-To:

- Chain a multiple of stitches (e.g., 12 + 2).
- Work increases and decreases strategically to form peaks and valleys.

5. EXPLORING COLORWORK TECHNIQUES

Adding color to your crochet projects enhances their visual appeal. Here are some beginner-friendly techniques for working with multiple colors:

1. Stripes: Simply switch yarn colors at the end of a row to create horizontal stripes.

2. Tapestry Crochet: Work with two or more colors in the same row, carrying the unused yarn along the back of your work.

3. Granny Squares with Color Changes: Use different colors for each round of a granny square to create a vibrant patchwork effect.

6. Planning and Executing a Textured Project

Now that you've learned about textured stitches and patterns, it's time to put them into practice. Let's plan a textured scarf project.

Textured Scarf Pattern

Materials Needed:

- Worsted weight yarn in two colors.
- 6.0mm (J/10) crochet hook.

Pattern:

- Foundation Row: Ch 22.
- Row 1: Work 1 sc in each chain across. Turn.
- Row 2: Alternate 1 FPdc and 1 BPdc across the row. Turn.

- Row 3: Work 1 sc in each stitch across. Turn.
- Row 4: Repeat Row 2, but start with BPdc instead of FPdc.

Repeat Rows 2–4 until the scarf reaches your desired length, alternating colors every four rows.

7. Tips for Success with Patterns and Textures

- .Practice Before Starting: Create small swatches to practice new stitches and techniques before incorporating them into a larger project.
- Use Contrast: When working with multiple colors, choose contrasting shades to highlight textures and patterns.
- Count Stitches Regularly: Textured stitches can be tricky; counting ensures you stay on track.
- Work Slowly: Focus on accuracy and consistency rather than speed,

especially when learning new techniques.

8. Troubleshooting Challenges in Textured Work

Uneven Stitches

- Cause: Inconsistent tension or incorrect placement of stitches.
- Solution: Practice maintaining even tension and carefully follow the pattern instructions.

Confusing Pattern Charts

- Cause: : Difficulty understanding symbols or chart layout.
- Solution:: Use written instructions alongside the chart and highlight each row as you complete it.

Yarn Tangles in Colorwork

- Cause:: Carrying multiple yarns without organizing them.

- Solution:: Keep yarns separated and untwist them regularly.

9. Expanding Your Creativity

Once you're comfortable with textured stitches and patterns, you can explore more advanced techniques, such as:

- Cables: Create intricate braids and twists using front and back post stitches.
- Lacework: Use chains and open spaces to create delicate, airy designs.
- 3D Designs: Combine bobbles, popcorns, and other textured stitches to form flowers, leaves, and other shapes.

10. Looking Ahead

Mastering patterns, textures, and stitch variations is a significant milestone in your crochet journey. With these skills, you can take on projects like blankets, garments, and decorative items that showcase your creativity and expertise. In the next chapter, we'll explore advanced techniques like shaping, joining, and creating seamless pieces. Exploring Patterns, Textures, and Stitch Variations. By incorporating these techniques into your work, you'll unlock endless possibilities for creative expression.

CHAPTER 5

PATTERNS, TECHNIQUES, TEXTURES

Now that you've mastered basic crochet stitches, it's time to build on those skills by exploring patterns, techniques, and textures. This chapter will guide you through reading and understanding crochet patterns, working in rows versus rounds, creating shapes, and introducing texture stitches that can elevate your projects. By the end, you'll have the tools to follow a variety of patterns and add dimension to your crochet work.

1 READING CROCHET PATTERNS

Crochet patterns serve as roadmaps for your projects. At first glance, they may seem intimidating, but understanding the language and structure of a pattern will make them easy to follow.

Anatomy of a Crochet Pattern

Most crochet patterns include the following components:

- Materials : A list of tools and yarn you'll need, including hook size and yarn weight.
- Gauge : A guide to the number of stitches and rows per inch to ensure your project matches the intended size.
- Abbreviations: Patterns use shorthand for stitches (e.g., sc for single crochet, dc for double crochet). Always check the key provided in the pattern.
- Instructions: Step-by-step directions to complete the project.
- Diagrams/Charts: Some patterns include visual charts that represent stitches with symbols.

Common Abbreviations and Symbols

Here are some commonly used abbreviations:

- ch: chain
- sc: single crochet
- dc: double crochet
- hdc: half double crochet
- sl st: slip stitch
- st: stitch
- yo: yarn over

rep: repeat

Example Instruction:
"Row 1: Ch 12, sc in 2nd ch from hook, sc across, turn (11 sc)."
This means
1. Chain 12.
2. Work a single crochet into the second chain from the hook.
3. Single crochet into each remaining chain.
4. Turn your work at the end of the row.
You'll have 11 stitches total.

Tips for Following Patterns

- Read Ahead: Familiarize yourself with the entire pattern before starting.
- Mark Your Place: Use sticky notes or highlighters to track your progress.
- Practice with Simple Patterns: Start with beginner-friendly projects, such as dishcloths or scarves, before tackling advanced designs.

2 WORKING IN ROWS VS. ROUNDS

Crochet projects are typically worked in either rows or rounds, each with its own unique technique and application.

Working in Rows

- Definitions: Working in rows involves creating a flat fabric by turning your work at the end of each row.
- Application : Ideal for blankets, scarves, and rectangular or square projects.
- Techniques :
    1. Start with a foundation chain.

2. Work stitches across the chain.
3. Turn your work at the end of the row and continue back across.

Tip: Use a turning chain at the start of each row to bring your hook to the correct height for the next row (e.g., ch 1 for single crochet, ch 3 for double crochet).

Working in Rounds

- Definition : Working in rounds involves crocheting in a circular pattern, either by joining at the end of each round or working continuously in a spiral.
- Application : Ideal for hats, amigurumi, doilies, and circular motifs.
- Techniques:
    1. Start with a magic ring (or chain 4 and join to form a ring).
    2. Crochet into the ring or around previous rounds.
    3. Close the round with a slip stitch or continue spiraling.

Tip: Use stitch markers to keep track of the beginning of each round, especially when working in spirals.

3 CREATING BASIC SHAPES

Understanding how to create basic shapes is essential for building complex designs. These shapes include squares, circles, and triangles.

Squares
This are commonly made using rows of stitches. The granny square, a classic crochet motif, is made by working in rounds.
- Granny Square Basics:
    1. Start with a magic ring or ch 4 and join.
    2. Work clusters of double crochets, separated by chain spaces, to create the square.

Circles

- Circle are created by increasing stitches in each round to maintain a flat shape.

Basic Circle Pattern:
1. Start with a magic ring.
2. Work 6 single crochets into the ring (Round 1).
3. Double the number of stitches in the next round (12 stitches total).
4. Continue increasing evenly in each round.

Triangles

- Triangles can be made by starting with a wide base and decreasing stitches in each row or by increasing from a point.

Basic Triangle Pattern:
- Start with a foundation chain.
- Work stitches across the chain, decreasing 1 stitch per row.

4 ADDING TEXTURE WITH STITCHES

Textured stitches add depth and dimension to your projects, making them visually appealing and more interesting to crochet.

Bobble Stitch

The bobble stitch creates raised, rounded clusters that add a playful texture.

Steps:
- Yarn over, insert hook into the stitch, yarn over, and pull up a loop.
- Repeat the process until you have 5 loops on the hook.
- Yarn over and pull through all 5 loops.

Shell Stitch

- •The shell stitch creates a fan-like pattern that's often used in decorative borders

Steps:
- Work multiple double crochets into the same stitch (e.g., 5 dc in one stitch).
- Skip a few stitches, then repeat.

Puff Stitch
- The puff stitch is similar to the bobble but softer and less dense.

Steps:
- Yarn over, insert hook into the stitch, yarn over, and pull up a loop.
- Repeat until you have several loops on the hook.
- Yarn over and pull through all loops.

Cluster Stitch

- A cluster stitch involves partially completing several stitches and closing them together.

Steps:
- Yarn over, insert hook into the stitch, yarn over, and pull up a loop.
- Partially complete the stitch, leaving the last loop on the hook.
- Repeat for the desired number of stitches, then yarn over and pull through all loops.

5 COMBINING PATTERNS AND TEXTURES

Once you're comfortable with various stitches, you can combine them to create intricate patterns and textures. For example:

- Alternating rows of bobble stitches and single crochet creates a playful, raised design.
- Mixing shell stitches with double crochets adds a lacy, elegant look.

6 ADVANCED TECHNIQUES

Color Changes

Switching colors can add stripes, patterns, or motifs to your projects.

Steps:
- Stop before completing the last stitch of the current color.
- Yarn over with the new color and pull through to complete the stitch.

Working with Multiple Strands

- Using multiple strands of yarn creates a thicker fabric or gradient effects.
- Hold two or more strands together as you crochet, using a larger hook to accommodate the thickness.

Tapestry Crochet

- Tapestry crochet involves carrying multiple colors of yarn and working them into the stitches to create patterns.
- Keep the unused yarn behind your work and switch colors as needed.

CHAPTER 6

CRAFTING CROCHET PROJECTS FOR EVERY SKILL LEVEL

This chapter focuses on the exciting journey of crafting crochet projects, ranging from beginner-friendly designs to advanced pieces that challenge your skills. By learning to plan, execute, and personalize projects, you'll gain confidence in your creativity while building a library of handmade items. With detailed guidance, this chapter helps you take your knowledge of stitches, patterns, and textures and apply it to real-world projects.

1 THE BASICS OF PLANNING CROCHET PROJECTS

Before you pick up your hook, thoughtful planning is essential to ensure the success of any project.

Choosing a Project

Start by selecting a project that matches your skill level and personal interests. For example:

- Beginner: Dishcloths, scarves, or coasters that use basic stitches.
- Intermediate: Hats, shawls, or small stuffed toys (amigurumi) that incorporate shaping and patterns.
- Advanced: Blankets, intricate lacework, or garments requiring detailed instructions and texture techniques.

Gathering Materials

Ensure you have all the necessary materials before starting. Key considerations include:

Yarn:

- Choose the appropriate weight and fiber type for your project

(e.g., cotton for dishcloths, wool for winter wear).
- Check the pattern's yarn recommendations or use a substitute with a similar weight and texture.

Hook:
- Use the hook size suggested in the pattern or adjust to achieve the correct gauge.

Notions:
- Items like stitch markers, scissors, a yarn needle, and a tape measure are often needed.

Understanding Gauge

Gauge measures the number of stitches and rows per inch in your crochet fabric.

- Patterns typically provide a gauge swatch to match.

Steps to Check Gauge:

- Crochet a small sample using the pattern's stitch and hook size.
- Measure your stitches and rows against the pattern's gauge.
- Adjust your hook size (smaller for tighter stitches, larger for looser ones) until your gauge matches.

Tip: Skipping the gauge swatch can lead to sizing issues, especially for garments.

2 BEGINNER PROJECTS: BUILDING CONFIDENCE

Let's explore beginner-friendly projects that use simple stitches and techniques.

Dishcloths

Dishcloths are small, practical, and ideal for practicing basic stitches.

- Pattern Example:
- Foundation: Chain 20.

- Rows 1-15: Single crochet across, turn.
- Fasten off and weave in ends.
- Customization: Add stripes by changing colors or use textured stitches like the moss stitch (alternating single crochet and chains).

Scarves

Scarves are versatile projects that let you experiment with length, width, and texture.

- Pattern Example:
- Foundation: Chain 200 (or desired length).
- Row 1: Double crochet in the fourth chain from the hook and across.
- Rows 2-10: Double crochet across.
- Add fringe for a decorative touch.

Coasters

Round or square coasters provide an opportunity to practice working in rows or rounds.

- Round Coaster Pattern:
- Round 1: Create a magic ring, work 6 single crochets into the ring, and join with a slip stitch.
- Round 2: Work 2 single crochets into each stitch (12 stitches total).
- Round 3: Single crochet, 2 single crochets in next stitch, repeat around (18 stitches total.

3 INTERMEDIATE PROJECTS: EXPANDING YOUR SKILLS

Once you're comfortable with the basics, move on to projects that incorporate shaping, patterns, and multiple techniques.

Hats

Crocheted hats introduce shaping techniques like increases and decreases.
- Basic Beanie Pattern:
- Round 1: Create a magic ring and work 10 double crochets into the ring.
- Round 2: Work 2 double crochets in each stitch (20 stitches).
- Round 3: Double crochet in next stitch, 2 double crochets in the next stitch, repeat around (30 stitches).
- Continue increasing until the crown reaches the desired size, then work even rounds for the body of the hat.

Shawls

Shawls are larger projects that often feature openwork patterns and intricate stitch combinations.
- Triangle Shawl Pattern:

- Row 1: Chain 4, work 3 double crochets into the fourth chain from the hook.
- Row 2: Chain 3 (counts as the first double crochet), double crochet in the same stitch, work 1 double crochet in each stitch across, ending with 2 double crochets in the last stitch.
- Repeat Row 2, increasing at the beginning and end of each row, until the shawl reaches the desired size.

Amigurumi

Amigurumi (crocheted stuffed toys) requires working in continuous rounds and precise shaping.

- Basic Ball Pattern:

- Round 1: Magic ring, work 6 single crochets into the ring.
- Round 2: Work 2 single crochets in each stitch (12 stitches).
- Rounds 3-6: Single crochet evenly.
- Round 7: Single crochet, single crochet two together (sc2tog), repeat around.
- Stuff the ball with fiberfill and close with a slip stitch.

4. ADVANCED PROJECTS: PUSHING YOUR LIMITS

Advanced projects challenge your creativity and technical skills with detailed patterns, intricate stitches, and precise shaping.

Blankets
Large, complex blankets often feature motifs, colorwork, or textured stitches.

- Granny Square Blanket:
- Make multiple granny squares using different color combinations.
- Join the squares together using slip stitches or whipstitching.
- Add a border by working rounds of single crochet around the entire blanket.

Garments

Crocheted sweaters, cardigans, and dresses require attention to gauge, shaping, and assembly.

- Top-Down Sweater Pattern:
- Start with a yoke, increasing evenly to create the neckline.
- Separate the stitches for the sleeves and body.
- Work the body in rows or rounds, adding shaping as needed.

Lacework

Lace projects, such as doilies or table runners, use fine yarn and intricate patterns.

- Doily Pattern:
- Begin with a magic ring.
- Work rounds of chain spaces and double crochets, following a chart or written instructions.

5 CUSTOMIZING YOUR PROJECTS

Personalization adds a unique touch to your work.

Adjusting Size

- Increase or decrease the number of stitches in your foundation chain or rows.
- Use a thicker yarn or larger hook for a bigger project, or finer yarn and a smaller hook for a smaller result.

Adding Embellishments

- Edging: Add decorative borders, such as picots or scallops, to finish your work.
- Appliqués: Crochet small shapes (e.g., flowers, hearts) and attach them to your project.

Incorporating Colorwork

- Stripes, tapestry crochet, and intarsia allow you to introduce vibrant patterns.

6 TROUBLESHOOTING AND FINISHING TECHNIQUES

Fixing Mistakes

- If you notice an error, gently unravel your stitches to the point of the mistake and start again.
- Use lifelines (a piece of contrasting yarn threaded through your stitches) for

complex patterns to make unraveling easier.

Blocking

Blocking helps your crochet pieces achieve the correct shape and size.

- Wet Blocking: Soak your piece, shape it, and pin it in place to dry.
- Steam Blocking: Use a steam iron to gently shape and flatten your work.

Weaving in Ends

- Use a yarn needle to weave loose ends into the back of your work.

Guides you through creating crochet projects for every skill level, from beginner-friendly dishcloths to advanced lacework and garments. By learning to plan, customize, and troubleshoot your projects, you'll become a versatile crocheter capable of bringing your creative visions to life.

CHAPTER 7

CARING FOR CROCHET CREATIONS AND SHARING YOUR CRAFT

As you progress in your crochet journey, one of the most rewarding aspects is seeing your creations come to life and sharing them with others. Whether it's a handmade gift, a piece for sale, or something to cherish in your own home, it's essential to know how to care for your crochet items and how to share your work effectively. In this chapter, we'll dive into techniques for maintaining crochet pieces, tips for gifting and selling your creations, and ways to join the crochet community.

1 CARING FOR CROCHET ITEMS

Handmade crochet creations can last for years if properly maintained. From washing to storing, every step contributes to preserving their beauty and functionality.

Washing Crochet Items
The washing process varies based on the yarn material and the project's purpose.

Step 1: Identify the Fiber

- Natural Fibers (e.g., wool, cotton): These require gentle handling. Wool is particularly delicate and may shrink or felt if exposed to high heat or agitation.
- Synthetic Fibers (e.g., acrylic, polyester): These are more durable and can usually withstand machine washing.
- Blended Fibers: Follow the care instructions for the most delicate fiber in the blend.

Step 2: Handwashing

Handwashing is the safest method for most crochet items.

- Fill a basin with lukewarm water and a mild detergent or wool wash.
- Submerge the item and gently swish it around. Avoid wringing or twisting, as this can distort the stitches.
- Rinse thoroughly with clean water.

Step 3: Machine Washing
If the yarn label indicates that machine washing is safe:

- Use a gentle cycle with cold or lukewarm water.
- Place the crochet item in a mesh laundry bag to prevent snagging.
- Use a mild detergent designed for delicates.

Step 4: Drying

- Lay the item flat on a clean, dry towel to maintain its shape.
- Reshape the piece as needed and allow it to air dry.
- Avoid hanging crochet items, as this can cause them to stretch out.

STORING CROCHET ITEMS

Proper storage prevents damage from moisture, pests, or mishandling.

Tips for Long-Term Storage
- Clean Before Storing: Wash and thoroughly dry your items to prevent stains or odors.
- Avoid Direct Sunlight: Prolonged exposure to sunlight can fade yarn colors.

- Use Breathable Containers: Store items in cotton bags or plastic bins with ventilation holes to prevent mildew.
- Add Protection Against Pests: Place cedar balls, lavender sachets, or moth repellent in storage containers.

Organizing Crochet Items

- Label storage containers with project names or descriptions.
- Fold larger items like blankets neatly to save space.

REPAIRING CROCHET ITEMS

Even well-cared-for crochet pieces can develop snags, holes, or loose stitches over time.

- Fixing a Snag: Use a crochet hook to pull the snag back into

place from the wrong side of the fabric.
- Patching Holes: Crochet a small patch using the same yarn and stitch pattern, then sew it over the hole.
- Reinforcing Edges: Add a new border to strengthen worn edges.

2 GIFTING CROCHET CREATIONS

Handmade crochet gifts are thoughtful and personal. Whether you're creating something for a special occasion or as a token of appreciation, the following tips will help you craft meaningful gifts.

Choosing the Right Project

Select a project that suits the recipient's preferences and needs.

- For Babies: Soft blankets, booties, or stuffed animals.

- For Friends: Cozy scarves, hats, or tote bags.
- For Home: Decorative pillows, table runners, or coasters.

Customizing Gifts

Personalize your crochet gift to make it unique:

- Colors: Use the recipient's favorite colors.
- Patterns: Choose motifs that reflect their personality or interests.
- Monograms: Add initials or names with surface crochet or appliqué.

Presentation Ideas

A beautifully presented gift enhances its impact.

- Wrap the item in tissue paper and place it in a decorative box.

- Attach a handmade tag with care instructions and a personal note.
- Include a small yarn sample in case repairs are needed in the future.

3 SELLING YOUR CROCHET WORK

Turning your hobby into a business can be a fulfilling way to share your craft. Whether you sell at local markets or online, preparation and marketing are key to success.

SETTING UP YOUR CROCHET BUSINESS

1. Decide What to Sell

Focus on products that highlight your skills and appeal to your target audience.

- Popular items include hats, baby blankets, market bags, and home décor.
- Consider seasonal trends, such as scarves in winter or lightweight shawls in summer.

2. Price Your Work Fairly

Factor in the cost of materials, the time spent crocheting, and a profit margin.
- A common formula: (Cost of Materials + Time x Hourly Rate) x Markup = Price.
- Research similar products to ensure your prices are competitive.

3. Build a Brand

Create a cohesive brand identity, including a logo, color palette, and tagline.

- Use consistent branding across business cards, social media, and packaging.

SELLING ONLINE

Online platforms offer access to a global audience.

Popular Platforms
- Etsy: Ideal for handmade items and crafts.
- Shopify: Allows for creating your own online store.
- Social Media: Use Instagram and Facebook to showcase your work and connect with customers.

Photography Tips
- Use natural lighting and a clean background.
- Include close-up shots to highlight texture and detail.

- Show your items in use, such as a blanket draped over a couch or a hat worn by a model.

SELLING LOCALLY

Local markets, craft fairs, and boutiques are excellent venues for selling your work.

- Prepare an Inventory: Bring a range of products and have extras on hand.
- Create an Engaging Display: Use props, baskets, or racks to showcase your items.
- Network with Customers: Hand out business cards and encourage repeat buyers.

4 JOINING THE CROCHET COMMUNITY

The crochet community is vibrant and supportive, offering opportunities to learn, connect, and inspire others.

Local Groups and Classes

Many communities have crochet clubs, classes, or workshops where you can meet fellow enthusiasts.

- Search for groups at local craft stores, libraries, or community centers.
- Consider teaching a class to share your skills and give back to the community.

Online Communities

Social media and forums are excellent places to share your work, ask for advice, and find inspiration.

- Instagram: Use hashtags like #crochetcommunity and #crochetlove to reach other crocheters.
- Ravelry: A popular platform for sharing patterns, projects, and tips.

- YouTube: Watch tutorials or start your own channel to teach others.

Participating in Crochet-Alongs (CALs)
A Crochet-Along is a group activity where participants work on the same project simultaneously, sharing progress and tips.

- Look for CALs hosted by designers, yarn companies, or online groups.
- Engage with others through forums or social media to stay motivated.

Caring for your crochet items and sharing your creations—whether as gifts, for sale, or within the crochet community—adds depth to your crafting journey. With the skills and knowledge you've gained in this book, you're ready to take your passion for crochet to new heights. Keep exploring, experimenting, and enjoying the art of crochet, and let your creativity inspire others along the way.

CHAPTER 8

TROUBLESHOOTING COMMON CROCHET PROBLEMS

Even the most experienced crocheters encounter challenges from time to time. Crochet is an intricate craft that requires focus, patience, and practice, so mistakes are inevitable—especially as you take on more complex patterns. Chapter 8 focuses on troubleshooting common problems you might face during your projects, helping you identify errors, avoid frustration, and correct your work with confidence.By the end of this chapter, you'll be equipped to solve problems such as uneven stitches, curling fabric, and yarn tangles. You'll also learn preventive techniques to minimize errors and how to handle common frustrations.

1. WHY MISTAKES HAPPEN IN CROCHET

Before we dive into specific problems, it's important to understand why mistakes occur in crochet. Here are some common causes:

- Inconsistent Tension: Your grip on the yarn and hook might be too loose or too tight, leading to uneven stitches.
- Misreading Patterns: Skipping steps, misinterpreting

abbreviations, or overlooking details can result in errors.
- Distractions: Crocheting in a busy or noisy environment can make it harder to focus, leading to mistakes.
- Lack of Experience: As a beginner or when trying new techniques, errors are part of the learning process.

Mistakes are a natural part of crochet and should be seen as opportunities to improve. With practice and patience, you'll develop the skills to troubleshoot and fix any issues that arise.

2. COMMON CROCHET PROBLEMS AND HOW TO FIX THEM

Problem 1: Uneven Stitches

Symptoms: Your stitches are inconsistent in size, making the fabric appear bumpy or uneven.

Causes:

- Tension is too tight or too loose.
- Inconsistent yarn feeding through your fingers.
- Incorrect stitch placement.

Solutions:

- Practice Maintaining Tension: Hold the yarn firmly but not too tightly. Practice with simple rows of single crochet to develop consistency.
- Count Your Stitches: Use a stitch marker or count after each row to ensure you haven't accidentally added or missed stitches.
- Check Your Grip: Adjust how you hold your yarn and hook for better control.

Problem 2: Curling Fabric

Symptoms: The edges of your project curl up or under, making the fabric difficult to work with.

Causes:

- Tension is too tight.
- Incorrect foundation chain.
- Using the wrong hook size for the yarn weight.

Solutions:

- Check Your Hook Size: Use a larger hook to loosen your stitches if the fabric curls.
- Adjust Your Foundation Chain: Ensure the foundation chain isn't too tight; try working the chain with a larger hook.
- Block the Fabric: For finished projects, use steam blocking or wet blocking to flatten the fabric.

Problem 3: Uneven Edges

Symptoms: Your project's edges are not straight and appear jagged or slanted.

Causes:

- Adding or missing stitches at the end of rows.
- Inconsistent turning chains.

Solutions:

- Use Stitch Markers: Mark the first and last stitch of each row to avoid skipping them.
- Follow Turning Chain Guidelines: Always chain the correct number at the start of each row, depending on the stitch you're using.
- Count Regularly: Count your stitches at the end of every row to ensure accuracy.

Problem 4: Holes in the Fabric

Symptoms: Your work has unexpected gaps or holes that disrupt the pattern.

Causes:

- Missing stitches or skipping steps in the pattern.
- Accidental yarn-overs.

Solutions:

- Check the Pattern: Revisit the instructions to confirm you're following the correct steps.
- Redo the Affected Area: Frog (unravel) the row or section with the hole and redo it.
- Prevent Future Errors: Keep track of your progress using stitch markers or row counters.

Problem 5: Yarn Splitting

Symptoms: The yarn separates into strands while crocheting, making it difficult to form clean stitches.

Causes:

- Using a hook that's too sharp or small.
- Working too tightly.
- Poor-quality yarn.

Solutions:

- Switch Hooks: Use a smoother or larger hook to prevent splitting.
- Improve Tension: Loosen your grip on the yarn for smoother stitches.
- Choose the Right Yarn: Opt for high-quality yarns with a smooth, even texture.

Problem 6: Tangled Yarn

Symptoms: Your yarn becomes knotted or tangled, slowing down your progress.

Causes:

- Pulling from the wrong end of the skein.

- Storing yarn improperly.

Solutions:

- Work from the Center-Pull End: Many yarns are designed with a center-pull strand to prevent tangling.
- Use a Yarn Bowl or Bag: Keep your yarn contained and untangled as you work.
- Untangle Carefully: If a knot forms, work slowly and gently to loosen it rather than pulling.

3 DEALING WITH FRUSTRATION IN CROCHET

Crochet can be a relaxing and meditative hobby, but it's easy to feel frustrated when things go wrong. Here's how to stay calm and enjoy the process:

- Step Away: If you're feeling overwhelmed, take a break and return to your project later with fresh eyes.
- Celebrate Progress: Focus on how far you've come rather than fixating on mistakes.
- Learn from Mistakes: Each error is an opportunity to grow and improve your skills.
- Seek Support: Join online crochet communities or local groups to share your challenges and successes.

6. LEARNING TO EMBRACE IMPERFECTION

Crochet is a skill that takes time to master, and perfection isn't the goal. Handmade items have character and uniqueness that no machine can replicate. Embrace the quirks and imperfections in your work as a testament to your effort and creativity.

7. MOVING FORWARD AND BUILDING CONFIDENCE

As you troubleshoot and solve crochet problems, you'll gain confidence in your abilities. Remember that every mistake you correct is a step toward becoming a more skilled and resourceful crocheter.

CONCLUSION

Crocheting is more than a craft—it's a creative expression, a skillful art, and a deeply rewarding pastime. From the first chain stitch to intricate patterns and complex designs, the journey of learning and mastering crochet offers endless opportunities for growth and satisfaction. What starts as a simple loop of yarn can transform into beautiful, functional creations that carry the warmth and care of handmade artistry. One of the most remarkable aspects of crochet is its accessibility. With just a hook, some yarn, and a bit of patience, anyone can learn the basics. It's a craft that encourages experimentation, enabling beginners to create simple projects like scarves or dishcloths while allowing seasoned crocheters to tackle intricate garments, lacework, or large-scale blankets. Each project builds upon foundational techniques, opening doors to explore new stitches, textures, and patterns.

Crochet also serves as a bridge between creativity and mindfulness. The rhythmic motion of stitching has a meditative quality, offering a sense of calm and focus. For many, crochet becomes a therapeutic outlet—a way to unwind, reduce stress, and channel emotions into something tangible. The satisfaction of completing a project, no matter how small, fosters a sense of accomplishment and pride. Beyond its personal benefits, crochet connects people across generations and cultures. It carries a rich history, with techniques and traditions passed down through time. Today, it continues to bring people together in local groups, online communities, and collaborative events like Crochet-Alongs. Sharing tips, patterns, and projects strengthens bonds within the crochet community, creating a supportive and inspiring environment for all skill levels.

Crocheting also empowers individuals to create unique and meaningful items. Whether crafting a personalized gift, contributing to charity, or starting a small business, crochet allows makers to leave their mark on the world. The ability to customize colors, materials, and designs makes each piece a reflection of the creator's vision and effort. Handmade crochet items carry a special significance, evoking thoughtfulness, care, and individuality in a way that mass-produced goods cannot replicate. As crochet evolves with modern trends and innovations, it remains rooted in its timeless appeal. From traditional motifs to contemporary patterns, the craft continues to adapt, blending heritage with creativity. The versatility of crochet ensures its relevance in the modern world, where makers can explore everything from sustainable crafting to digital design tools for pattern creation.

Made in the USA
Monee, IL
06 March 2025